So Say We All, "B is for Bravery!"

THE FOUR MENARDS

So Say We All, "B" is for Bravery

By: The Four Menards

Illustrated by: Gil So

Designed by: Darlene Swanson · www.van-garde.com

ISBN: 978-0-9891734-6-9 (hardcover)
978-0-9891734-7-6 (paperback)

Published by The Four Menards Publishing, Asheville, NC 28816

TheFourMenards@gmail.com

Printed by Lightning Source, Inc., La Vergne, TN 37086

The Four Menards

A Wrinkle in Rhyme

This book is dedicated to the victims
of the Sandy Hook Elementary School
and all of their friends and families.
<u>All proceeds</u> from this inspirational account
are donated to the relief of those who
have lost loved ones, and to safety measures
to prevent future tragedies of this nature.

A group of children left the Earth
this bright December day;

An issue-riddled gunman
came and took their lives away.

Some elementary school staff
on the scene have also died,

Chaotic hell and torment running
rampant countrywide.

With Christmas coming in eleven days,
it shook the lives,

Of devastated parents, brothers,
sisters, husbands, wives.

The monumental grief left people
silent in the street;

Though strangers to the victims,
tears were shed in sad defeat.

Emotions rattled every heart,
from seeking faith to doubt,

The human mind could hardly
even start to sort this out.

Two sets of parents held together
and appealed to God —

They got a grand response
out in a field where angels trod!

For late the night it happened,
they could not withstand the pain,

And wandered back behind the school,
"God, help us to stay sane!"

Now neither couple understood
that they were summoned there,

But hugged each other and
engaged in tearful, shouting prayer.

So Heaven's hosts were present
for a time that served them well,

As they were sent by God, Himself,
to help them through their hell!

The gentle angels nodded
to the four despairing souls;

One father, Paul, now on his knees,
was seen by night patrols.

The squad car pulled up
but was halted by an angel's hand,

The officers bowed deeply, whispering,
"Yes, we understand."

Then they were fixed upon their spot
but felt no need for fear,

For both sensed that the Lord, Himself,
had brought these people here.

The mother of Paul's child yelled,
"You took our only kid!"

Then added, "Are You up there, God?!
— Then tell me what I did!

You let that gunman kill my child
and he gets off Scott Free!"

The woman shuddered through her tears
— "You took my son from me!"

The second father, Tom, sobbed,
"Lord, she'll never see her bike,

They were to be their Christmas gifts;
we bought them both alike.

And what are we supposed to
tell her older sister, Lord?

That we have been defrauded,
by the One we all adored?"

The broken voices carried on,
they cried in such despair,

"And what about their guardian angels,
why were they not there?!"

The anger and the sadness rang
as every cry was heard,

But for the moment, Heaven's hosts
spoke not a single word.

Then all four parents fell down
in a cold exhausted state,

One cop looked toward an angel,
"Will you speak if we all wait?"

The couples held each other,
shaking from fatigue and loss,

The dark sky filled with brilliant stars;
a moon bow raced across.

The leading angel softly spoke
and showered them with calm,

While all six people realized
that they didn't sense alarm.

"The six of you will carry back
the hope we will provide,

For God, Himself, will reassure you;
He will be your guide.

When loved ones are removed from us,
it can't be understood;

As mortals, you have not yet gained
the knowledge so you could.

God knows this, and He will provide
the strength to get you through;

That's why you have been led here
and we have been sent to you.

We'll answer all your questions, now,
and try to ease your grief,

And as we pray together,
we will help you find relief."

The group of six was silent
as the angel softly spoke,

Except for Tom's wife; Molly's mom,
who sobbed, "Well, that's a joke!"

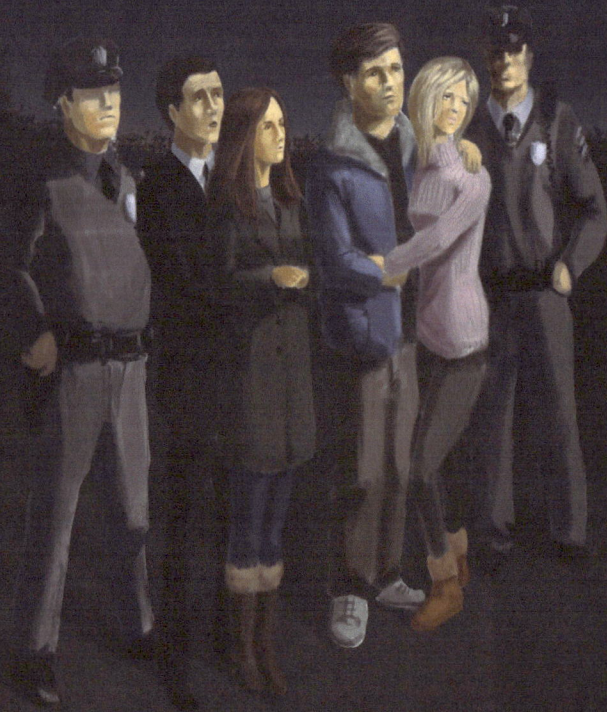

Tom pulled her closer
as her worn out body shook with pain,

"Keep holding her," the angel smiled,
"this is no easy gain."

The officers sat with the four,
each took a couple now,

"We're going to get through this,"
whispered one, "they'll show us how!"

The angel started: "<u>Item One</u>:
The 'gunman got off free….'.

So say we all, 'Oh no!
Not quite- despite what you can see!'

<u>Item Two</u>: Your broken hearts
imagine your child's harms.

So say we all, 'They <u>instantly</u>
left in God's mighty arms.'

Again regardless of the looks,
please try to lose your fear;

For these small children were protected
and removed from here.

Item Three: The guardian angels
that God should provide -

So say we all, 'from firsthand sight,
were at each victim's side.'

Now <u>Item Four:</u> The memories
of your children who have gone,

So say we all — 'continue these —
your children carry on.'

They play in Heaven as we speak,
and know of total bliss;

Perhaps God looked at Earth
and thought, 'They'll have much more than this!'

Then called them home to be with Him,
and live in His great care,

So keep right on remembering them —
they're waiting for you there.

Just close your eyes and send your love;
we're with you till the end —

We'll personally deliver
every hug and kiss you send!

19

The same is true for staff members,
who came Home with them too;

Deliveries are free of charge;
we'll have them sent right through!

<u>Item Five</u>: Regarding all regrets
if faith was shaken,

So say we all, 'God knows your pain
and you won't be forsaken!

He understands your limits,
and He loves you just the same,

So never feel one second
that you can't call out His name!'"

The field lit up — there came a voice —
among the stars above;

The sound was so remarkable —
so filled with power and love!

And He appeared — Breathtaking Sight!
Said, "Come and walk with Me,

There's something that I'd like
for every one of you to see."

Escorted by His angels,
He moved several yards away,

Then raised His hand toward Heaven, saying,
"Move toward Me, then stay."

The six were stunned by what they saw
— an opening in the sky;

The wonder was too much to grasp,
and all of them knew why!

The site before them was too
overwhelming to endure,

The mortals knew at once,
they must be viewing Heaven's shore!

Such gorgeous flowers, waterfalls,
the colors of the grounds;

The peaceful, sheer magnificence;
the happiest of sounds.

The officers, amazed beyond
the words they couldn't say,

Just marveled from the field they stood in,
and began to pray!

In peaceful rest, both sets of parents
softly sobbed with joy,

For now they knew the whereabouts
of their young girl and boy.

"And Tom," God smiled toward his wife,
"I'm taking Molly's bike,

So tell her sister, Kelly,
that she rides the one alike,

Rejoicing that her sister has come
Home for now with Me,

Until you're reunited
when it's time for you to be."

25

The Great I Am continued, with a smile and a wink,

"And Paul, I did not take your only child as you may think,

For I have sent another one as you will find out soon,

So Mom, rejoice! You're carrying a child beneath this moon!

As far as anger and revenge, I ask that you will see,

That I am very capable — so leave that up to Me."

Then Molly's mom moved toward Him
as she felt her heart strings tug,

"I am so sorry, Abba," she said,
giving Him a hug.

"Go now," He smiled as angels sang,
"and pass this night along,

To all of those who hurt and grieve
because they were done wrong.

Tell each of them their loved ones
will all carry on just fine,

And they will wait in Heaven,
just beyond these stars that shine."

The mortals, both exhausted
and refreshed, went home that night.

As Tom pulled into his garage,
he tripped the ceiling light.

His wife said, "My mom's fast asleep,
so let's turn nothing on."

Tom smiled as tears streamed down his cheeks,
for Molly's bike was gone!

But Grandma met them in the hall;
"I've called the cops," she said,

"Somebody's entered your garage!
They took a bike, then fled!"

The officers pulled up and laughed
in tears of great relief,

And Grandma was the first to hear
the story of the Thief!

God bless all of you and keep you in
His mighty hand! Your loved ones are
not as far off as you may have thought!

"B, is for Bravery"

A teacher wakes up early,
when the sun's not risen yet,

And thinks of what her kids
will learn today – the alphabet.

She thinks of each one's tiny face;
each student's little smile;

The sound of their small sneakers
as they run across the tile.

She's gathering her books up now,
and hurries out the door,

In hopes the children find cheer
in the Christmas pin she wore.

She's teaching them a song today
about the continents,

And one about the different ways
to count out fifty cents!

Their lesson's interrupted
by some gun shots and a shout;

Out in the hall, there's panic;
people running all about.

She tells her students to stay calm,
and races to the door;

She turns the lock, her eyes sprint
to the cupboards on the floor.

The gunman kicked the door in,
and then rushed up to her desk;

She stood heroically; thought fast,
and put him to the test!

Her children were all hidden
in the cupboards all around,

She'd told them that she loved them;
told them not to make a sound.

The killer stood in anger,
asking where the students were;

She calmly said, "They're in the gym."
He turned his gun on her.

She heard no screams and crying,
no expressions of despair;

For in that instant, she looked up
and saw the Father there.

He told her that He loved her
and would keep her from all harm,

Then lifted her above the scene,
wrapped in His mighty arm.

"But what about my students, God?
I have to see them through!"

He whispered, "I brought angels here,
to handle that for you.

You've placed yourself between
My children and the killer's gun,

And seen them right to safety,
honey — every single one!

You've done a most amazing job;
I'm very proud of you,

The little ones you gave your life for,
now will make it through.

Because of you, their parents
get to take them home tonight;

They'll watch them play in safety now,
in grateful love and light.

And each day forward, they will look
to Heaven, and they'll pray,

For that courageous teacher,
who has saved them all this way.

The other little ones and staff,
who leave the Earth today,

Will join us in this journey Home,
where they will safely stay.

Those parents and their families
will be settled once they see,

That all of those who lost their lives,
have come back Home with Me."

He had a twinkle in His eye
and leaned in close to say,

"You didn't notice, but you wore
two wings to school today."

He motioned toward the classroom
and the pictures on the walls,

"It's not by chance I'd sent
My very best to walk these halls."

As they arrived on Heaven's shore,
the group knew total love;

They rushed into each other's arms,
beyond the clouds above;

Among the gorgeous, peaceful
settings where the angels stay,

In grand delight and pleasure,
that they came to live that way.

The holidays came by and went,
and everyone lived on,

But not a day goes by
without the thoughts of those who'd gone.

The class learned all the continents
by singing their same song,

The
Continents Singers

And even though they didn't hear her,
guess who sang along?

They didn't see the angel chewing gum against the wall,

Nor see the angel in the playground stop a child's fall.

A little girl who cried, now found a cupcake in her lunch,

Since mother didn't put it there,
they all had just a hunch!

And while the staff came back to visit Earth
that sunny day,

The twenty kids who left with them,
stayed back with God to play.

They hugged Him and they ran around,
delighted with each game.

"So twenty kids at once," He laughed,
"We'll never be the same!"

God bless all of you and keep you in
His mighty hand! Your loved ones are not
as far away as you may have thought!

Love to all, The Four Menards

The Four Menards

A Wrinkle in Rhyme

The Four Menards are a family based in Asheville, North Carolina. They write colorful children's books in verse with entertaining, strong, moral messages.

A special thanks to Gil So for his illustrations and to Darlene Swanson for her graphic design, which reflect their heartfelt concern for all of the victims of the Sandy Hook Elementary School and their families.

thefourmenards@gmail.com

www.ingramcontent.com/pod-product-compliance
Lightning Source LLC
Chambersburg PA
CBHW041755050426
42443CB00022B/1